MOROCCO
Land of the Setting Sun

Cover Model: Satarra Johnson-Kidd
Cover Design: Nadine C. Duncan
Interior Design: Nadine C. Duncan

ISBN: 979-8-9889182-0-2
ISBN: 979-8-9889182-1-9 (ePub)

2nd Edition, August 2023
Travel Guide Series, Volume VIII
Printed in the United States of America

Published in the United States by:
Traveling Black Women™
Grace Royal International, LLC
Atlanta, GA 30316

www.travelingblackwomen.com

Diary of a Traveling Black Woman:
A Guide to International Travel

"Mini Travel Guide Series"
Volume VIII - Morocco
2nd Edition

Morocco:
Land of the Setting Sun

Satarra Johnson-Kidd

The Traveling Black Women Network
Grace Royal International, LLC
Atlanta, GA

Diary of a Traveling Black Women: A Guide to International Travel

Mini Travel Guide Series

Dubai, Abu Dhabi & The 5 Other Emirates You Didn't Know About

Jamaica: Likkle, but Tallawah!

Studying Abroad for Black Women

Iceland: Nature, Nurture, & Adventure

Solo Travel: Try It At Least Once!

And more...

Contents

To Art

Hello!
My name is Satarra...

I'm just a regular chocolate princess from Japan, studying Spanish in Honolulu, Hawaii. I have spent most of my young adult years traveling the world. In the past year and a half, I have been to France, Morocco, and Peru. Out of all the countries I've been to, Morocco is the one that I will remember forever!

Ever since I could remember I've always wanted to travel. So, when I found out that I got accepted to the study abroad program in Morocco for three months, I was beyond excited. As an International Business major, this opportunity fit perfectly. I chose this program and this country specifically because

I was able to study business and culture there. I had always been interested in Northern African culture, so I knew that Morocco was the place for me to go.

Most people would be scared to visit Morocco alone as a Black female traveler. But not me!! (To be fair, I'm not really scared of anything, ha!). I was too excited to think about anything else. All I could think about was getting there and the new culture I would be able to experience! So on June 19, 2018, I found myself alone in Rabat, Morocco, not knowing that I was embarking on a trip that I would remember for the rest of my life!

I write this guide with the intentions of helping all my fellow chocolate beauties navigate their way through Morocco! I hope that my quick guide makes you feel like you can take a well-planned and well-prepared trip to Morocco.

Enjoy!

@mila.illustrated

What to Know

Trip Preparation

Based on the traveling I have done in my life, I think it's safe to say that one should always be prepared for the worst when it comes to airports. You may already know this but, the number one thing you should always be when it comes to international flights is EARLY!!

International flights are always a bit more stressful than domestic flights because of all the security procedures you have to go through. Every airport is different but I recommend showing up to any international flight at least two hours early.

FYI: Believe it or not, some airlines--such as Iberia Airlines that flies into Casablanca through Spain-- will not honor TSA Precheck. Therefore, regardless of your precheck status, you may want to arrive as early as possible.

Depending on the airline, sometimes you can check into flights online and other times you cannot. When I went to Morocco, I flew with

Delta and I couldn't check into an international flight online. If you ARE able to check into your flight online, make sure that you do so and either print your ticket or have the boarding pass on your phone.

You also want to make sure that you keep your passport accessible while moving throughout the airport. It makes life so much easier!

Airport Ready
Checklist:

	Your passport
	2 photocopies of your passport
	A soft copy of your passport in "the Cloud"
	2 alternate forms of ID
	Cash
	Debit/Credit Card
	A backup phone charger
	A hard copy of your boarding pass or confirmation
	Easily accessible boarding pass or confirmation on your phone
	Snacks for the plane
	A light jacket
	Compression Socks
	Comfortable shoes

Airport Information:

Morocco has a number of airports, but there are two popular international airports that I would recommend flying into: Casablanca (CMN) and Marrakesh (RAK). These airports are huge, modern, and efficient!

Visas:

If you are staying in Morocco for more than 90 days, you will need a visa. If you are traveling to Morocco for less than 30 days, then you can simply get a visa on arrival (stamp) at the airport. Stay up to date by checking with the American and Moroccan embassies to see if you will or will not require a Visa to travel to Morocco.

Vaccinations:

To travel to Morocco you may need certain vaccines. If you're like me, then you HATE vaccines and shots more than anything in the world! But the way I look at it, this is just a small price to pay in order to travel to such a beautiful country!

The *suggested* vaccinations for Morocco are: DTP, Hepatitis A, Hepatitis B, MMR, Rabies, Schistosomiasis, Tuberculosis (required), and Typhoid fever. Before you decide to get vaccinated, I recommend talking with your doctor to figure out what vaccines they might recommend personally for you. You will find that some people do not get vaccinated at all.

Staying Connected:

Before leaving your home country, decide what the best option would be for you to stay connected to your friends and family back home. You can opt for an international plan with your current phone service, use Wifi calling apps (when Wifi is available), or simply purchase a local SIM card for your unlocked phone when you arrive in Morocco. You will see shops selling "Maroc Telecom" and "Inwi" SIM cards nearly everywhere. They are easy to purchase and have great signal. You can top up your phone and data almost every where, even at small shops in the mountains.

You'll be happy to know that most places, including restaurants in the mountains, are equipped with Wifi. Although the Wifi is not always the best, it is typically available. Therefore, opting to disconnect until you have access to Wifi is a viable option.

Depending on where your family and job is located in the world, staying connected can be tough. While I was in Morocco, my family was living in Washington, DC. There is a five-hour time difference between Rabat and DC. With this time difference, I would have to plan different times to talk with my family. This is something I advise you do ahead of time. Figure out what the time difference is between Morocco and your home city, and then try to come up with a schedule to check in with friends and family. Fortunately, everyone in my family has an iPhone. I was able to easily Facetime my family using the Free Wifi at my home in Morocco.

Packing:

When you pack for your trip you should always make sure that you have your essentials (medicine, clothes, sunscreen, etc.), but make sure you don't over pack! I tend to over pack and never leave enough room for all the souvenirs I end up buying.

To prevent you from making the same mistake that I made, here's a list of everything you should bring when visiting Morocco:

- **Modest Clothing:**
  It is so important to be respectful of the Moroccan culture despite the weather. Morocco is a Muslim country and women are expected to cover up. You don't have to be covered from head to toe, but it is important not to show too much skin, or wear anything that could be considered too tight. It can get very hot in Morocco, so modest, loose fitting clothing is your best bet for dealing with the weather and respecting

cultural norms.

- **Umbrella & Waterproof Clothing:**
  The rainy season lives up to its name. If you plan to travel during the rainy season (November-March), make sure to pack an umbrella and some type of waterproof gear. Don't be shy about lugging an umbrella around, because you WILL need it.

- **Comfy Shoes for the Medina (Market):**
  For those of you who are luxury travelers and like to look like Queens whenever you travel, the Medina in Morocco is not the place for that. You will want to wear comfortable shoes. The sidewalks are not stable, there are people and puddles everywhere, and you will be walking a lot (there is minimal vehicular access). There are plenty of places in Morocco to wear heels, the Medina is definitely not one of them.

- Light clothing for during the day & warm clothing for the night:

  During the day the sun is excruciating, so you should pack light clothing, and give that melanin some time to absorb the sun with breathable fabrics. At night, when it gets pretty cool, bring warmer clothing or at least a jacket.

- Bug Repellent:

  The spiders, mosquitoes, and bees in Morocco are NO JOKE. They don't care about who you are or where you're from. The bugs will bite and sting you with no problem. Trust me, I know! The bugs bit me the WHOLE time I was there, so pack a lot of bug repellent.

- Sunscreen:

  The hot Moroccan sun does not play, and neither does our skin! Contrary to popular belief, Black women DO sun-burn and we CAN get skin cancer. Be sure to pack a lot of sunscreen. I know

many of us think that our lovely chocolate melanin protects us from the sun
naturally, but that's not 100% true. We
still need to consider packing 30+ sunscreen to protect our skin from the sun.

• Adapter:
Morocco uses the European outlets
with the two round prongs. I'd suggest
having an universal travel adapter with
USB outlets.

• Back Up Phone Charger:
If you plan on using your phone to take
photos or videos, you will definitely
need a back up charger! Aside from
that, even if you opt to disconnect, it's
smart to have a charged device accessible!

What to Expect

Cultural Norms

Morocco is a Muslim country. While there is a small percentage of citizens who are not Muslim, the expectations for how to dress and behave are a lot different from the Western cultural norms of the United States and most European countries. For women especially, modest clothing is advised. You will see women usually cover up their arms and legs in addition to their hair.

- Religion
  One of the many things that makes Morocco significant and beautiful is Islam. If you have anything against Islam or do not like the religion, I recommend not visiting Morocco. It is advised that you do not publicly speak negatively of Islam. Whenever you walk into a place or greet someone, it is custom that you say "Salam" to greet them. It is a greeting that not only means "hello," but acknowledges peace between you and

the other person.

- ## Ramadan

  Expect to hear the call to prayer five times per day. If you plan on traveling through Morocco during the month of Ramadan, then you can count on most stores and restaurants being closed. In fact, I don't recommend traveling to Morocco during Ramadan if you are not Muslim--a lot of businesses are closed (including the markets), and your options of things to do will be limited. You would end up having a much different experience visiting during Ramadan than you would during any other time of the year. So, be sure to check the calendar before going and make the best decision for yourself.

- ## Sex

  I must reiterate, Morocco is not like the United States and it is important to be respectful of the culture. In reality you can say what you want to say there, but there are many things--including conversations--that are against cultural norms. For example, people do not talk about sex in public. If you are having a conversation with your friends and the topic of sex comes up, I advise you not to speak too loudly as sex isn't something that is discussed freely. It seems silly for me to mention this, but it is such a common part of our Western culture that we may not realize the different implications an overheard conversation may have.

- Pork
  Everything you eat and every food that you buy will not contain pork or pork products (like gelatin). If you are the type of person who enjoys pork, I'm sorry! In the Quran, pork is prohibited. All the other food options available in Morocco, however, are absolutely delicious. My personal favorite was the couscous. Couscous is

served every Friday in Morocco as a part of their culture. I promise if you try it, you'll fall in love. It is incredibly delicious. You'll forget all about pork.

- Language
  Moroccans speak Arabic, French, Berber, Spanish, and English. Arabic is the national language while French is the language that was imposed during the French colonization. While many prefer to speak Arabic, most Moroccans speak both Arabic and French fluently. In the city of Chefchaouen, however, you will find that a large part of the local population speak Spanish. This is because of the geographical and historical influence of the Spanish in that region. The Bedouin residents of Morocco speak Berber. As of April 2019, this community has been pushing to have Morocco recognize Berber as an official language of Morocco.

• Squatting Pan Toilets

In **some** public restrooms you will find the squatting pan toilets like the one pictured below. Do not be alarmed! They are actually pretty easy to use! These toilets literally require you to squat and release. If there is no flushing capability, you will find that there is a bucket for water and a low faucet nearby. After using the squatting pan, you are expected to fill the bucket with water and pour it down the toilet. Remember not to flush any tissue! There should be a small garbage nearby for that!

Getting Around

The best way to get around in Morocco is by **foot, taxi, train, and bus**. The bus is the least recommended because it can be unreliable and as a woman, it can feel unsafe. It is the best route, however, to get to cities like Chefchaouen (the Blue City) where there is no train access.

Taxi

The "Petit Taxi" is the number one way to get around within a city. They are usually smaller cars like Peuguots or Fiats. The taxis in each city are a specific color. The vibrancy of the color and the size of the car allows the taxis to easily stand out. In each city, it will be easy to spot a fleet of petit taxis that are all the same color waiting outside of the airport, train station, or bus station.

Taxis are usually a variation of red, blue, yellow, green, or white. For example, in Rabat and Chefchaouen you will see blue Petit Taxis, in Casablanca and Fez they will be red, and in Marrakesh an orangish beige called ochre.

The downside to taking a taxi in Morocco is that the price is never set. When you take a local taxi, you will need to negotiate the price before hopping in. The petit taxis all have meters that often do not work (although the jury is still out on that!) If the driver knows that you are a tourist, they will most likely raise the price for you. The price they tell you the first time is most likely not the average price. To be on the safe side, ask a local you can trust (i.e. Riad manager, tour operator, hotel doorman) to talk to the taxi driver for you. They can assist with negotiation and would be able to better gauge the quality and safety of the driver.

Train

Locals will tell you that the infrastructure in Morocco has changed drastically over the last few years--largely due to tourism. Their modern train system is the best (and cheapest) way to travel between cities. The trains are clean, comfortable, and efficient. The train stations in larger cities often have small shopping centers with a variety of restaurants and free wifi.

Purchasing train tickets are extremely simple. The schedules are listed online as well as at the train station. I would advise reviewing the schedule online before arriving at the station. Each train station has a ticket counter as well as ticket kiosk. The kiosk has an English option and takes Visa and Master card. You also have the option to purchase your tickets online!

Bus

The bus is the least recommended but can still be a viable option when traveling between cities. As previously stated, cities like Chefchaouen are not accessible by train. For example, in order to access Chefchaouen (without a private driver from a larger city like Marrakesh or Casablanca), you can take the 2-hour train to Tangier and hop on the bus for about another hour or so. Bus tickets can also be purchased online, but their schedules aren't as reliable as the train.

Climate

When I lived in Morocco, I stayed in Rabat. Rabat was hot. There is no way around it. It was very hot and humid. I can't stress that enough, I felt like I was going to melt. I couldn't walk 15 minutes, without being drenched in sweat. If you go during the summer season, which is June to September, you can expect extremely hot weather. This is the season where you should pack light, bring a lot of sunscreen, and buy a lot of water. I would also like to add that most Moroccan cities are crowded, and the crowds will make you feel much hotter. Keep that in mind if you travel during the summer.

The months of November to January are known as the rainy season. During this season you want to make sure to bring your umbrella (or poncho for easy packing). The winter season is from December to March. It can get around 65 degrees during the day (not that cold) to around 40 degrees at night. The winter season isn't like winter season in the United States, so if anything you might want to bring a light jacket, but you will not need a heavy coat.

If you plan on venturing out to the Sahara, you can expect to experience several different climates in one day. As you ascend the mountains, you'll find that some areas are below freezing, while others feel like the sun is sitting in your lap. The best way to dress for this sort of experience is in layers!

Money

The currency for Morocco is the Moroccan Dirham. As of September 2019, one US dollar is equivalent to approximately 9.66 Moroccan Dirhams. When you arrive at the airport, change a small amount of your money (I'd recommend $50 - $100) in the airport to get you started. However, I will not recommend changing all your spending money at the airport because the fees are much cheaper at banks outside of the airport.

I would also recommend getting cash and *not* the Moroccan credit card some exchange places offer you. That temporary credit card seems like a great idea as credit cards are widely accepted, but it will 1) Charge you a small fee with every transaction 2) Not be honored in a number of places 3) Leave you with a balance that is too low to swipe or withdraw.

Make sure to contact your bank before leaving the US so that they are aware of your movements. If you need to withdraw cash, check the symbols on the ATM and on the back of your card to ensure that your card is compatible with the ATM. The ATMs in busy areas like a square or medina are usually the most reliable.

Accommodations

Accommodations in Morocco are reasonably priced and easy to find online. I would recommend staying at a Riad while in Morocco. Although hotels and hotel chains are available, a Riad gives you the authentic Moroccan experience at a great price. To choose the best Riad, simply read the reviews on TripAdvisor. Riad owners and managers take their ratings on TripAdvisor very seriously.

Most Riads are unassuming, and even questionable, from the outside. But, once you are inside, you enter a home-like atmosphere with several floors of private rooms and en-suite bathrooms in a courtyard like setting. At registration, you are often greeted with the famous Moroccan Mint Tea and the utmost hospitality. The architecture is unlike anything else in the world. Riad managers are always willing to assist you with getting a cab or ensuring you know how to get around on foot.

Most Riads also include breakfast. Not the

continental and stale coffee type of breakfast, but a large spread prepared by the Riad's chef. Once you let the manager know your schedule for the following day, he will make sure your breakfast is prepared fresh when you are awake and ready.

Pros/ Cons
For Black Women

Just like in life in general, there are many pros and cons to consider as a Black Woman. Although sometimes it can *seem* like there are more cons than pros, there is nothing in the world that I would trade in for being a Black Woman. You'd be surprised where Black Girl Magic can get you!

Racism & Colorism

For the most part Moroccan people are very nice people, but the intersection of race and gender is not a concept to be taken lightly. I have to be honest in saying that Morocco is one of the countries that you really have to watch out for when it comes to racism and body objectification.

In Morocco, some people don't even like to be identified as African (even though Morocco is clearly in Africa). When I was in Rabat, I faced a lot of racism from people as well as objectification of my skin and body. Colorism can be a problem too. In some parts of Morocco, people with light skin, European features, blonde hair, and blue eyes are the ideal "look." The darker you are and the more "African" your features are, the greater your chances are of running into racism.

In my experience, there were a number of times that I was with my friends (all Black), and the servers at restaurants treated us horribly. In some cases, we were the last to be served, and in others we were ignored completely.

Don't get me wrong, overall, I had a really good time in Morocco. But I do want Black women traveling to Morocco to be aware that while every situation may be different, racism in Morocco is definitely a thing.

Harassment

As far as body objectification goes, me being a Black woman is the first thing they note when making catcalls. Verbal harassment against women in general is horrible in Morocco, but, I would say the harassment against Black women is even worse. Everywhere that I would go, I constantly heard "Hey brown skin! Girl with the big butt! Blackie! Braids! Africa! Etc." I would constantly hear these things being called at me. I ignored it for the most part, but it got annoying after a while.

Even worse, when I would meet men, whether in the club or at a restaurant, they would always point out the fact how they have never "slept" with a Black girl. They would talk about my body and how they don't normally have girls that have body types like mine. This might not entirely be a Morocco thing, but this can happen wherever you are one of the only Black Women in a situation. Regardless, it made me extremely uncomfortable.

Hair Care

If you are only going for a short vacation, I would recommend a low maintenance style like braids, twists, or faux locs. When it comes to hair care, other than Moroccan Argan oil, I couldn't really find any hair products that would work for my 4b natural hair.

Positive Attention

Pros of being a Black woman in Morocco, is the fact that you're a Black woman in Morocco. As Black women, we are among the most beautiful and intriguing races in the world. When we travel we attract a lot of attention due to our melanin and deep features. Just like there is a lot of negative attention, there is a lot of positive attention. I did get a number of people telling me how beautiful I was, as well as other people happy to see someone like me traveling. Whenever I'm abroad, whether it be Japan, Peru, or Morocco, and I see Traveling Black Women, I can't explain to you the satisfaction I feel in my heart.

Regardless of where we go, we risk facing racism and unfavorable reactions to our bodies. That is why it's so important to know your worth and beauty as a Black woman.

You are not there to be anyone's stereotype.

Packing

List

What to Do

The possibilities of things to do in Morocco is endless. In the following section I'll give you an overview of what you can do in Morocco. **You can go to the beach, the desert, the city, and the mountains all in one trip.** There are many different agencies that you can book your activities through, but I recommend doing some research before booking any activity. Booking in advance using sites like Viator is your best bet as established tour operators take their ratings on TripAdvisor (Viator's parent company) very seriously!

When I went to Morocco, I wanted to try something new everyday. It didn't matter if I was sick or broke, I just wanted to get out because I was so excited to be there. Not everything requires a lot of money, even walking along the beach can be something free and very adventurous. I can guarantee that in Morocco you'll never be bored because there are so many options.

Here are a few suggestions to add to your itinerary.
I'll conclude with a sample itinerary!

Bouznika Beach

Personally, when I travel to another country I don't like to do any activities that I can do at home. The first thing I did when I went to Morocco was ride a camel on Bouznika beach. Bouznika Beach is located approximately 35 minutes from Rabat and 40 minutes from Casablanca. As a tourist favorite, it is popular for surfing, camel riding, and playing golf! Definitely a check for the ~~bucket~~ life list.

Chefchaouen – "The Blue Pearl"

Chefchaouen *(pronounced 'Chef sho wen')* is a quaint, unique city in the northern part of Morocco in the Rif Mountains. Known as the Blue Pearl of Morocco, Chefchaouen is one of the safest cities in Morocco for a woman to explore on her own. You can spend a full day in Chefchaouen simply exploring the city... And that's really all you need. A guide wasn't necessary for Chefchaouen as it is pretty safe, filled with tourists, and easy to get around. If you have a local SIM, your phone GPS will come in pretty handy if you get turned around. It is the perfect city to truly get lost in! Look for a Riad nearby that is within walking distance to the medina.

FYI, it is not as easy to access Chefchaouen as it may seem (unless you are going with a tour group). It is much cheaper to hop on the train to Fez or Tangier, take a 2-3 hour scenic bus ride to the city, book a Riad for a night, and explore on your own. One thing to note, however, is that you will find a number of shops selling Argan Oil and leather. Beware of fake Argan Oil and goods made in China. The best place to purchase souvenirs is actually on the road to Desert Camping where you can stop at Argan Oil Cooperatives, and local shops with hand-made goods.

Desert Camping

Desert camping in the Moroccan Desert is an amazing experience. The vastness of the sand dunes, the depth and dark of the night sky, and the breathtaking sunset are indescribable. It is during this experience that you will understand why Morocco is known as the "Land of the Setting Sun."

A visit to Morocco is not complete with the desert camping experience. There are a number of companies in Morocco that offer Desert Camping tours that take tourists through the Atlas Mountains and into Erg Chebbi sand dunes of the Sahara Desert. Each tour and tour company offer slightly different itineraries, so be sure to read the descriptions and reviews carefully. If you feel indecisive, you can always reach out in the Traveling Black Women online community.

Depending on when you go, you may also experience a wide range of temperatures on the way to the Sahara desert from the city. As a matter of fact, the journey to the Sahara was equally (if not more) amazing due to the sites you can stop and visit along the way. Be sure to dress comfortably and in layers so that you are prepared for the temperature to drop as well as for the sun to beam down on you in the same day.

FYI, the camps are usually well established camp sites with fully functional bathrooms and electricity. The tents are relatively large with basic twin beds. Most tours encourage you to leave the bulk of your luggage in the Kasbah or Riad before meeting the camels. You only need to take with you a small bag or backpack with toiletries and a change of clothes. Depending on the number of nights that you are staying at the camp, the expectation is for you to shower when you return to the your hotel accommodations.

The camel ride to the camp is long and uncomfortable, but well worth it. Watching the sunset and sunrise while riding a camel through the desert feels surreal. If you grew up watching Aladdin, you can't help but hum Arabian nights to yourself.

Sample Desert Camping Itinerary
3 Days, 2 Nights

- Day One:
  Meet with the tour company and other
  tourists between 7AM and 8AM. Drive
  into the **Atlas Mountains** stopping at
  UNESCO sites like **Ait Ben Haddou**
  and various lookouts with panoramic
  views. The day usually concludes with
  dinner (included) and a stay at a kasbah (now a Moroccan hotel).

- Day Two:
  After breakfast at the kasbah, you'll
  drive out toward the **Erg Chebbi** dunes
  stopping for lunch and more scenic
  views. In the evening, you will arrive
  at another kasbah where you will leave
  the bulk of your belongings and pack
  a smaller bag or backpack to take on
  your trek into the Desert. After down-
  sizing, you will meet the caravan of
  camels that you will ride to the camp.
  Once you arrive at the camp, they'll be

dinner and entertainment waiting for you!

- Day Three:
  Wake up at sunrise and ride the camels back to the kasbah. Once you have showered and dressed, join the group for breakfast and head back to the city!

Fes (Fez)

The largest medina in the world is located in Fes, Morocco. A medina is a small city, historically behind a wall that is complete with vendors selling all types of food, clothes, shoes, perfumes, housewares, etc. It feels like an intricate maze, particularly in Fes. The best way to safely explore the intricacies of a large medina is to book a walking tour in advance. Fes is notorious for scammers attempting to assist visibly lost tourists. Book that tour in advance!

Fes was once considered the political, spiritual, and intellectual center of Morocco. In some ways, the locals still revere it as such. You will find that many of the goods found throughout Morocco are made in Fes. Because of this, it is very easy to get carried away while shopping! Set a budget before you begin exploring! If money isn't a thing, post offices (Post Maroc) are reliable and widely available to ship items back home that you don't want to take on the plane. Ask your Riad director or tour guide to assist at the Post Office if you aren't fluent in Arabic or French.

Tanneries

Fes is also known as the leather city! Any type of leather product you want or want made, can be found in Fes. The tanneries in Morocco are a sight to see and a smell to smell.

If you are vegan or have strong feelings toward the use of animals for manufactured goods, you will want to bypass the tanneries completely. The tanneries are not just leather shops, but also leather processing plants. The strong smells in tanneries come from the ammonia in bird poop that is used to process the shedding skin of animals.

In the view of the tanneries work space you will see animal skin being hung to dry, tubs of natural dye, and tubs of bird poop ammonia used to remove the fur from the animal skin. The smell is absolutely horrible.

The University of Al-Qarawiyyin

The University of Al-Qarawiyyin is noted as the oldest degree-granting university in the world as well as one of the largest mosques in Africa. You will see it spelled 101 different ways because of the translation into English. The university was founded around 859AD by a Tunisian woman. Yes, this means the oldest university in the world was founded by an African woman. Most of the university/mosque is off limits to non-Muslims. You can get a peek of the inside of some areas from several open, guarded doors.

The "Goat Tree"

My favorite attraction was traveling to the Southwest part of Morocco (Sous Valley) and seeing the tree goats perched in the Argania tree. If you're an animal lover like myself, I recommend it! The goats are drawn to the Argan fruit found in these trees. They are considered a valuable asset as their poop produces the highly sought after Argan nuts that are pressed to create Argan oil.

FYI, scammers are known to tie goats to trees to attract tourists wanting to take pictures. Look for authentic locations where goats are freely climbing the trees.

Hammam (Moroccan Bath)

Moroccan hammams are among the best spa experiences in the world. Hammams can be found easily throughout all Moroccan cities. They consist of a spa menu that includes full body scrubs and massages. Book a hammam as soon as you arrive and one before you leave to bring you trip full circle!

FYI, the expectations for the scrub is that you are completely naked and ready to be scrubbed from head to toe. There is no need to be shy or uncomfortable! Just stand there and relax!

Marrakesh

Marrakesh is arguably the most popular city in Morocco. This is the city you will see highlighted on Instagram the most. You will be able to see a clear distinction between the new medina and the old medina while touring Marrakesh.

The new medina is geared more toward American and European tourists. The old medina has a more authentic feel. Shop owners in the medina seem more aggressive in Marrakesh than the other cities. It is much more uncomfortable as a female traveler than the other cities--particularly in the Old Medina. With that said, mind your pockets and beware of "tour guides" and other scam artists lurking in the medina for confused looking tourists. Be stern. They will take the hint and keep it moving. "La Shukran," meaning "No! Thank you!" will quickly become your favorite phrase.

Nonetheless, there are a few attractions that are must sees throughout Marrakesh:

- Yves Saint Laurent Museum
  The famous Yves Saint Laurent Museum is adjacent to Jardin Marjorelle and the Berber Museum. The Jardin Marjorelle is noted for its beautiful garden and blue architecture trimmed in yellow. It is an IG favorite.

- **Djemaa el Fnaa Square**

  This square, or plaza, is among one of the more popular plazas to explore while in Marrakesh. The plaza is surrounded by a variety of shops, banks, and restaurants, while filled with street performers and street food. The square can be a great place to visit and take in the sites, but look out for pick pockets and scam artists!

- **Hotel vs. Riad**

  Popular hotels are widely available in Marrakesh. Riads however, are highly recommended as they are elegant, cheaper, and can give you the authentic Moroccan feel. When selecting a Riad, read the best review, the worst review, a few in the middle to get a good sense of what to expect. Reviewing the location is important as some surprisingly beautiful Riads can be found in dark alleyways.

Sample Backpacking Itinerary

Day 1: Arrival in Casablanca

Depending on where you are arriving from **Casablanca (CMN)** tends to be the cheaper airport to fly into. Casablanca is a pretty modernized city so there isn't much to see and do there beyond a city tour that includes the Hassan II Mosque (the largest Mosque in Africa and third largest Mosque in the world). Spend one night in Casablanca.

Day 2: Bouznika Beach

Bouznika beach is only 40 minutes outside of Casablanca. It is a great spot to relax and take in the landscape. If you want to get a little practice for your camel ride later in the week, check out the camels chilling on the beach. After a few hours at the beach, make your way to Rabat--only 35 minutes away.

Day 3: Moroccan Food Tour in Rabat

Rabat is an amazing city to explore. I'd spend 2 nights here as opposed to one. Here you can book the Moroccan Food Tour. The guide on this tour walks you through the medina and gives you a pretty rich history and background to what you are seeing, doing, and eating.

Day 4: The world's largest Medina in Fes

Hop on an early train to Fes from Rabat. Tickets are relatively inexpensive for the 4-hour ride. You can purchase tickets online (ONCF) or at the train station. This is referred to the country's cultural capital and the leather city.

Once you get to Fes, the most important destination that you should see is the Old Medina! To reach the Old Medina, it can be very confusing. I recommend booking a tour with a trusted tour company or tour guide. Remember, this is the best place to shop outside of the Co-Ops in the mountains. Spend an additional night if you need more shopping time. You can always mail your purchases back to the US.

Day 5: Travel to Chefchaouen (The Blue Pearl)

Hop on an afternoon train from Fes to Tangier. When you arrive in Tangier, take the bus from Tangier to Chefchaouen (two hour ride). This is a city that can't be skipped and a city that most people consider "Instagrammable." Spend at least one full day here, taking as many pictures as you can, as well as buying souvenirs in the Medina! I'd recommended spending 1-2 nights in Chefchaouen.

Day 6: Explore Chefchaouen

Spend the day exploring Chefchaouen and living your best instagram life!! This is the kind of city you can simply get lost in! Beware of purchasing fake goods like Argan Oil.

Day 7: Travel to Marrakesh

Take an early bus from Chefchaouen to Tangier. Be sure to book in advance because the buses aren't as frequent or reliable as the train--especially in Chefchaouen. Once in Tangier hop on the train to Marrakesh. Spend the night in Marrakesh. If you aren't too tired, head over for a stroll through Djemaa el Fnaa square.

Day 8 - 10: Desert Camping in the Sahara Desert (Merzouga)

This is best suited at the end of your trip as a grand finale of sorts. Visiting Merzouga/Sahara Desert is probably one of the biggest attractions that tourists travel to Morocco for. I highly recommend going!! Merzouga is a small town located in the desert and is a peaceful place to stay if you only want a desert experience. Refer back to page 62 for the sample desert camping itinerary!

Day 11: Head home or Explore Marrakesh

You will most likely return to Marrakesh pretty late after desert camping! I'd recommend flying home from Marrakesh (if you flew into a different city). If you have more time, explore Marrakesh!

Food Tour & Cooking Class

Morocco is the food-ie's delight. The best way to indulge your-self in the food cul-ture of Morocco is to take a street food tour and/or cooking class. Guided food tours allow you to learn your way around the mar-kets in the medina as well as what to look for with the expertise of a local. You are more like-ly to try different foods when you know what it is!

Cooking classes are also a delight as Moroc-co is a country full of exotic, delicious spices. A good cooking class will demonstrate how a concoction of Moroccan spices are used to create amazing dishes along with the impor-tance of color.

Cooking classes can be easy to find in any major city in Morocco. Some are hosted by private families, while others are hosted by restaurants and hotels. If you like to cook, this experience will inspire you to spice things up a little differently when you return home!

Nightlife

If you are looking for amazing and live nightlife in Morocco, then I recommend you go to either Marrakesh or Casablanca. These are places with a lot of clubs and bars. As part of the Islamic culture, you will not find alcohol to be widely available. However, Casablanca and Marrakesh are both modernized cities that cater to the whims of tourist. As a result, you will find a number of clubs, restaurants, and bars selling alcohol and playing pop music.

My personal experiences with clubs in Marrakesh are they are not at all like the clubs I'm used to back home. In DC, the clubs are predominantly Black, and there's a lot of rap, hip hop, and "twerk" music. In Marrakesh, the music they play at clubs are usually EDM or techno, with circus-like performance acts. So, even going to a club in Morocco can be an experience!

Enjoy your trip!

Diary

About the Author

Satarra Johnson-Kidd is an International Business graduate from Hawaii Pacific University. She current resides in the Washington, DC where she is the owner and curator of Arts in Color Curatorial. Each year Satarra tries to visit at least one new country.

@satarraleona

Work, Travel, Save, Repeat

TravelingBlackWomen.com
@travelingblackwomen

www.ingramcontent.com/pod-product-compliance
Lightning Source LLC
Chambersburg PA
CBHW040856120626
46551CB00001B/42

* 9 7 9 8 9 8 8 9 1 8 2 0 2 *